# DESIRE

## CAUGHT BY THE TAIL

PORTRAIT D L'AUTEUR

# PABLO PICASSO

# DESIRE
## CAUGHT BY THE TAIL

*Illustrated by the Author*

# *A Play*

*Translated from the French by*
*Bernard Frechtman*

The Citadel Press

New York

**FIRST PAPERBOUND EDITION, NOVEMBER, 1962**

Copyright 1949 by Philosophical Library
Manufactured in the United States of America
Published by The Citadel Press,
222 Park Avenue South, New York 3, N. Y.

WE offer a strange dish, *mi-figue, mi-raisin*. During the first winter of the German occupation of Paris, Picasso laid aside his brushes for three days and emerged with the present concoction. It was clearly a painter's recipe. The odour of oil which spreads through the play—literally, for which see the close of Act Four—is of oil of the atelier no less than of the cuisine. The congealed disrespectful will remark, "Three days? Obviously." Or, "It reflects the decline of French cuisine during the food crisis." This will exhaust sociological criticism. The reverent will marvel at this three days' wonder. But there are other alternatives than disrespect and reverence.

Add a Spanish chef a bit ill at ease with the ingredients of the French language, which, it must be observed, he abuses. The result is *Le Désir attrapé par la queue*, which title rendered literally as *Desire Caught by the Tail* is a reproduction in black and white of a painting, as the informed will agree; it should be a project of the uninformed to learn why.

The play is beyond criticism and likewise beyond those who seek more in it than a farcical creation of new objects and new relations. It does not invite comparison with *Hamlet* or *Phédre*, though it does with *Ubu Roi*. It says nothing of human destiny or the human condition. In an age which has discovered man with a capital M, it is gratifying to advise the reader that Picasso has nothing to say of man, nor of the universe. This in itself is a considerable achievement. In fact the characters are not even human. Nor, except for the Two Bow-wows, which articulate briefly, are they animal. This is a further achievement. The reader should note these matters.

*Amusez-vous bien.*

B. F.

# *CHARACTERS*

BIG FOOT

ONION

TART

THE COUSIN

ROUND END

THE TWO BOW-WOWS

SILENCE

FAT ANGUISH

SKINNY ANGUISH

THE CURTAINS

*Act One*

## SCENE I

### BIG FOOT

Onion, stop being funny. We had a bang-up time last night and we're all set to give our cousin a piece of our mind. We ought to explain once and for all the causes or consequences of our adulterous marriage. Its muddy soles and wrinkles must not be hidden from the gentleman rider, however respectful he may be of conventions.

### ROUND END

Just a minute, just a minute.

### BIG FOOT

No use, no use.

### TART

That'll do, that'll do, a little quiet and let me speak.

### BIG FOOT

All right.

### ROUND END

All right, all right.

### THE TWO BOW-WOWS

Gua, gua.

I wanted to say that if we want to come finally to some understanding on the matter of the price of the furniture and the renting of the villa, we'll have to—and with absolute perfect agreement—take Silence's suit off and put him naked into the soup which, by the way, is beginning to get cold at a mad rate.

FAT ANGUISH

I ask permission to speak.

SKINNY ANGUISH

Me too, me too.

SILENCE

Will you shut up!

ONION

The choice of this hotel as a meeting place, a walled-in public place such as this, is not yet made and we first have to examine with a microscope, bit by bit, the stray down of the subject which is still quite unsettled.

BIG FOOT

Don't hide yourself so cleverly behind the behind of the story which is of such great interest and distress to us all; the choice of witnesses is made and well made, by cracky! And as for us, we'll be quite happy to cut our pattern by the shadow cast by the bills owing to the landlord.

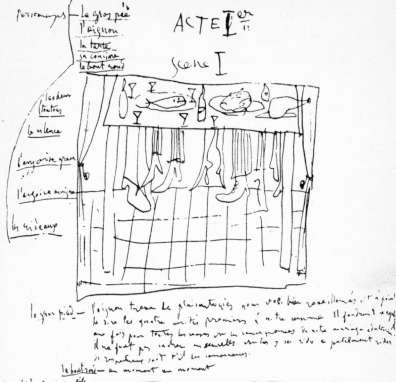

personnages — Le gros pied
l'oignon

la tarte
sa cousine
le bout rond

les deux toutous

le silence

l'angoisse grasse

l'angoisse maigre

les rideaux

ACTE I er II

scène I

le gros pied — l'oignon tâche de plaisanteries pour n'être bien remaillonnés et à point le rire les quatre unités premiers à notre comme Il faudraient accepte une fois pour toutes les usages ou les conséquences de notre mariage s'éclatent Il ne faut pas cacher ensemble cru les y se ride à patiellement rider il espérons soit s'il les commencens.

le bout rond — un moment un moment

le gros pied — inutile inutile

la tarte — mais en fin mais en fin au jour de d'âme et l'âge moi partie

le gros pied — bien

le bout rond — bon bon

les deux toutous — que—qué

le gros pied — je voulais dire que si vous voulons vous entendre en fin une page du plus de marbre et de la lessive de la ville et s'emfuit et s'en absolut prendrait accord lentablement tout le porte le silence se sens complet et le autre ma dans la soupe qu'autre pourrait comme à reposition et un vitre salle

l'angoisse grasse — je demande la parole — l'angoisse maigre — moi aussi moi aussi — le chœur—pratiques pour tous

[*taking off his clothes*]
Gosh, it's hot!

### THE COUSIN

I already put some coal on a little while ago, but it doesn't give any heat. It's a pain in the neck.

### ONION

We'll have to clean out that chimney tomorrow; it smokes.

### ROUND END

It would be better to build a younger one next year. That way—no more mice or cockroaches.

### TART

I prefer central heating; it's cleaner.

### SKINNY ANGUISH

How bored I am. . . .

### FAT ANGUISH

Shut up, we're guests here.

### ROUND END

To bye-byes, to bye-byes. Do you know what time it is? A quarter past two.

## SCENE II

[*Change of light: light of a storm.*]

### THE CURTAINS
[*Tossing about.*]
What a storm! What a night! A real certainly caressing night, a Chinese night, a pestilential night in Chinese porcelain. Thunderous night in my incongruous belly.
[*Laughing and blowing.*]

> [*Music of Saint-Saens: "La Danse Macabre." Underfoot, the rain starts falling on the floor and will-o'-thewisps run about the stage.*]

**Curtain.**

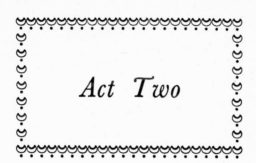

*Act Two*

## SCENE I

[*A corridor in Sordid's Hotel. The two feet of each guest are in front of the door of their room, writhing in pain.*]

THE TWO FEET OF ROOM 3

My chilblains, my chilblains, my chilblains.

THE TWO FEET OF ROOM 5

My chilblains, my chilblains.

THE TWO FEET OF ROOM 1

My chilblains, my chilblains, my chilblains.

THE TWO FEET OF ROOM 4

My chilblains, my chilblains, my chilblains.

THE TWO FEET OF ROOM 2

My chilblains, my chilblains, my chilblains.
[*The transparent doors light up and the dancing shadows of five monkeys eating carrots appear. Complete darkness.*]

## SCENE II

[*Same setting. Two hooded men bring an immense bath-tub full of soap-suds on the stage in front of the doors in the corridor. After a snatch of violin music from "Tosca", the heads of* BIG FOOT, ONION, TART, THE COUSIN, ROUND END, THE TWO BOW-WOWS, SILENCE, FAT ANGUISH, SKINNY ANGUISH, *and* THE CURTAINS *emerge from the bottom of the bath-tub.*]

#### TART

Nicely washed, nicely rinsed, clean, we are mirrors of ourselves and ready to start all over again tomorrow and every day with the same merry-go-round.

#### BIG FOOT

I see you, Tart.

#### ONION

I see you.

#### ROUND END

I see you, I see you, you little hussy.

#### BIG FOOT

[*addressing* TART]
You've got a shapely leg and a well-turned figure, the ridges of your eyebrows are maddening, and your

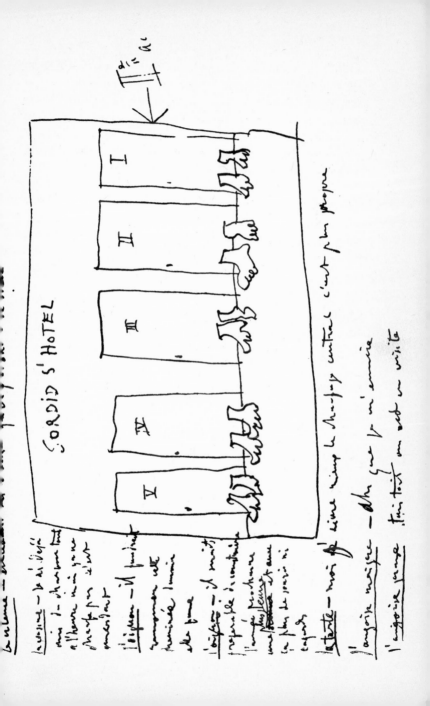

mouth is a nest of flowers, your hips a sofa, and the spring-seat of your lap a box at the bull-fights in the arena of Nimes, your buttocks a dish of baked beans, and your arms a shark-fin soup, and your . . . and your nest of swallows still the fire of swallow's-nest soup. But my dear, my ducky, and my pet, I'm in a dither, in a dither, in a dither, in a dither.

ONION

Old tart! Little trollope!

ROUND END

My dear fellow, where do you think you are, at home or in a brothel?

THE COUSIN

If you continue, I shall refuse to wash any more and shall go right away.

TART

Where's my soap? my soap? my soap?

BIG FOOT

The hussy!

ONION

Yes, the hussy!

TART

This soap smells good, this soap smells good.

[ 24 ]

Take your sweet-smelling soap! You know what you can do with it!

Lovely child, would you like me to rub you?

What a slut!

> [THE TWO BOW-WOWS, *barking, lick everybody; covered with soap-suds, they jump out of the bath-tub, and the bathers, dressed like everybody of that period, get out of the bath-tub.* TART *alone comes out, completely naked except for stockings. They bring baskets full of food, bottles of wine, table-cloths, napkins, knives and forks. They prepare a big picnic lunch. Some undertaker's mutes arrive with coffins into which they dump everybody, nail them up, and carry them off.*]

*Curtain.*

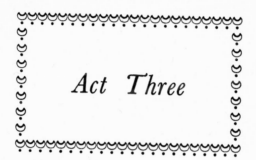

*Act Three*

## SCENE I

[*Black back-drop, wings and black carpet.*]

BIG FOOT

When you come to think of it, there's nothing like a
good mutton stew. But I like it better with onions, or
well done with wine, on a day of happiness full of snow,
by the meticulous and jealous care of my Hispano-
Mauresque Slav slave and albuminous servant and mistress,
melting into the fragrant architectures of the kitchen.
Apart from the pitch and the lime of her detached con-
siderations, there's nothing like her gaze and her chopped
flesh over the calm sea of her queenly movements. Her
bursts of temper, her warmth and her chill stuffed with
hate are nothing, right in the middle of the meal, but the
spur of desire interspersed with tenderness. The cold of
her nails turned against herself and the fiery points of her
icy lips on the straw of the dungeon-cell which thrown open
does not diminish the character of the scar of her wound.
The turned-up shirt of beauty, her embossed bosom
anchored to her bodice and the force of the tides of her
charms shake the golden powder of her gaze in the nooks
and crannies of the sink which stinks of the washing spread
out to dry at the window of her gaze sharpened on the
grindstone of her tangled hair. And if the Aeolian harp
of her filthy common dirty language and her laughs
irritate the shiny surface of this portrait, it is to her over-
large proportions and her disturbing propositions that she

[ 29 ]

owes this avalanche of homage. The spear of the bouquet of flowers that she plucks from the air as it passes by cries out in her hands the royal admiration of the victim. Crystallized into thought, the galloping pace of her love, the linen born in the morning in the fresh egg of her nudity clears the obstacle and falls panting on the bed. I carry those scars on my body; they are alive, they shout and sing and prevent me from catching the 8.45. The roses of her fingers smell of turpentine. When I listen at the ear of Silence and I see her eyes closing and spreading the perfume of her caresses, I light up the candles of sin, at the match-stick of her calls. The electric stove can take the blame.

## SCENE II

[*Knocking at the door.*]

### ROUND END

Anyone there?

### BIG FOOT

Come in!

### ROUND END

It's nice here, Big Foot, and what a good smell of roast boar! Good night, and I'm on my way. But while I was crossing the bridge of sighs I saw a light in your place and I dropped in to bring you your ticket for tonight's drawing of the national lottery.

### BIG FOOT

Thanks. Here's the money. That's the sort of luck I have this morning at my elevenses with figs—half-fig, half-grape, and so fresh. One more day and it's black glory.

### ROUND END

How cold!

### BIG FOOT

Want a glass of water? That'll warm up your inside. This business of renting a house preoccupies and saddens me. For if the landlord, good old fat Jules, is in agreement on the price and the maintenance costs, that pest of a

[ 31 ]

neighbour opposite bothers me. Her big cat does nothing but prowl around the cage of my mice and I see the time coming when the fish of the islands which I feed to them alive are going to be made into mincemeat and devoured by that stupid beast. My barrel-jumping frogs are in good health, but the aloe wine that I made is turning, and I no longer see the end of this winter without our being greeted by a bigger famine.

### ROUND END

The best thing to do would be to put a little dead mouse at the end of a solid fish-hook, and, letting the line trail gently at the end of a cane, lie in wait so that the big cat snaps at it. Kill him, skin him, cover him all over with feathers, teach him to sing and repair watches. After that, you can roast him and make yourself an herb broth.

### BIG FOOT

He who laughs last laughs best. With the cat dead, and she whom I love coming to wish me a Happy New Year, the house will shine like a lantern and the feasting will break all the violin and guitar strings.

### ROUND END

Madness! madness! madness! Men are mad. The scarf of the veil that hangs from the eyelashes of the shutters is wiping the pink clouds on the apple-coloured mirror of the sky which is already awakening at your window. I'm going out to the corner bistrot to claw off that bit of chocolate colour which is still prowling around in the black of its coffee. A very good morning to you, till tomorrow evening, see you later!

[*He leaves.*]

## SCENE III

[BIG FOOT *lies down on the floor in the middle of the* *stage and begins to snore. The* ANGUISHES, *the* COUSIN, *and* TART *enter from both sides of the stage.*]

SKINNY ANGUISH

[*looking at* BIG FOOT]

He is lovely, like a star. He is a dream repainted in water-colours on a pearl. His hair has the art of the complicated arabesques of the rooms of the Palace of the Alhambra and his complexion has the silvery tone of the bell which sounds the tango of the evening to my love-filled eard His whole body is filled with the light of a thousans. electric bulbs all lit up. His trousers are blown up with all the perfumes of Arabia. His hands are of transparent peach and pistachio ice-cream. The oysters of his eyes enclose the hanging gardens their mouths wide open to the gaze of his words and the colour of garlic-flavoured mayonnaise which encircles him sheds so gentle a light on his chest that the song of the birds that one hears clings to it like an octopus to the mast of a fishing smack which, in the eddyings of my blood sails in his image.

FAT ANGUISH

I'd like to have a go at him without his knowing it.

[ 34 ]

[*tears in her eyes*
I love him.

### THE COUSIN

I knew a gentleman in Chateauroux, an architect who wore glasses, who wanted to keep me. A very nice and very rich gentleman. He never wanted me to pay for my dinner and in the afternoon, between seven and eight o'clock, had his apéritif at the big café on the corner of the main street. It was he who taught me to carve a sole correctly. Afterwards, he left home for ever to live in an old historic castle. Well, I find that lying that way on the floor and sleeping, they look exactly alike.

### TART

[*throwing herself on him and weeping*
I love him, I love him.

[TART, *the* COUSIN, *and the two* ANGUISHES *each takes out a big pair of scissors and they begin to cut off locks of his hair until they've peeled his head like a Dutch cheese known as the 'death's head'. Through the slats of the Venetian blinds of the window, the whips of sunlight begin to strike the four women seated around* BIG FOOT.]

### TART

Ai ai ai ai ai ai ai. . . .

### THE COUSIN

Ai ai ai ai. . . .

### SKINNY ANGUISH

Ai ai ai ai ai. . . .

A a a a a a a a a a a. . . .
   [*And this continues for a good quarter of an hour.*]


### BIG FOOT

   [*dreamily*]
Icebergs are flowing down the bone of the marrow.


### THE COUSIN

Oh, isn't he handsome! Ai ai ai . . . who ai . . . oh!
who ai ai ai is ai ai ai ai . . . bo bo.


### FAT ANGUISH

A a a bo a a bo bo.

### TART

Ai ai I love him Ai ai love bobo ai ai ai love him ai ai
bo bo bo bo.

   [*They are covered with blood and fall to the floor in a
      faint.* THE CURTAINS, *opening their folds in front of
      this disastrous scene, immobilize their spite behind the
      expanse of the outspread cloth.*]


*Curtain.*

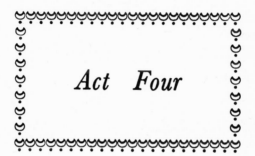

*Act Four*

[*Stamping of feet.*]

### TART

I'm going to win! I'm going to win! I'm going to win!

### THE COUSIN

Me too! Me too! Me too!

### FAT ANGUISH

I'll be first! I'll be first!

### BIG FOOT

I shall have the jack-pot!

### ROUND END

I shall get it!

### ONION

I always must be first and I shall be first!

### SILENCE

You'll see, you'll see!

### SKINNY ANGUISH

My little finger has told me!
[*The wheel of the lottery turns.*]

### THE COUSIN

7. What luck! I win the jack-pot!

24, plus 00.10 42. But I win the jack-pot too. That makes 249 thousand 00 89.

### FAT ANGUISH

9. That's my number that wins the jack-pot.

### TART

60, plus 200, and a thousand, and 007. I win the jack-pot too! I've always been lucky.

### BIG FOOT

4,449 by gosh! I'm a billionaire with the grand jack-pot!

### SILENCE

1,800. Farewell, misery, milk, eggs, and milk-maid! I'm master of the jack-pot.

### ROUND END

4,254. Jack-pot winner that I am, I congratulate me.

### THE COUSIN

0009. I'm the jack-pot winner! I'm the jack-pot winner! I'm the jack-pot winner!

### ONION

3,924. I win the jack-pot! That's right.

### FAT ANGUISH

11. The jack-pot is what I win!

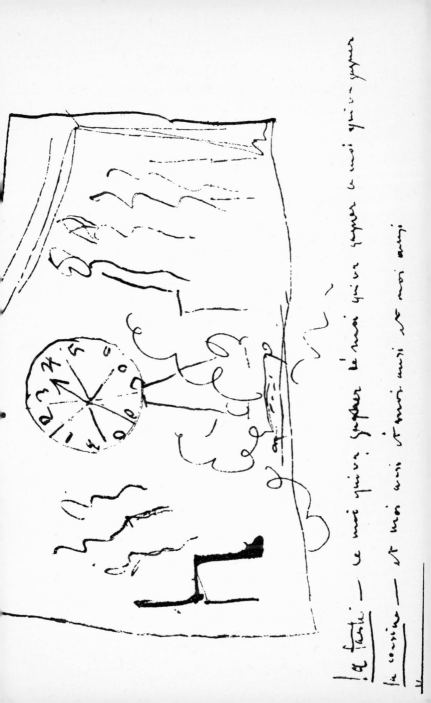

17,215. I've got the jack-pot everywhere!

THE CURTAINS

[*tossing about like lunatics*]

1. 2. 3. 4. We're winning jack-pots! We're winning jack-pots! We're winning jack-pots! we're winning jack-pots!

[*Great silence for a few minutes, during which, in the prompter's box, over a big fire and in a big pan, potatoes are seen, heard, and smelt frying in boiling oil; more and more, the smoke of the fried potatoes fills the hall to the point of complete suffocation.*]

*Curtain.*

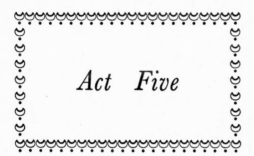

*Act  Five*

*[half stretched out on a camp bed, writing]*

"Fear of the moodiness of love and the moods of the caperings of rage. Gargle of the molten metal of her hair shrieking with pain all her joy at being possessed. Game of chance of the crystals which have been stuck on the melted butter of her equivocal gestures. The letter which follows step by step the word inscribed on the lunar calendar, hanging by its folds on the brambles bursts the egg which is filled with hatred and the tongues of flame of her will jointed into the paleness of the lily at the exact point where the exasperated lemon melts with delight. Double game of jacks painted in the red of the edging of her coat, the gum-arabic which trickles from her calm attitude shatters the harmony of the deafening noise of silence which has been caught in a trap.

"The reflection of her grimaces painted on the mirror which is open to all the winds aromatizes the hardness of her blood on the coldness of the flight of doves which receives it. The blackness of the ink which envelops the sun's rays of saliva which strike upon the anvil of the drawing obtained at the price of gold develops, in the needlepoint of the desire to take her in one's arms, one's acquired strength and the illegal means of achieving it. I run the risk of having her dead in my arms, full-blown and mad."

Love letter, if you like. The sooner written and the sooner torn up. Tomorrow or this evening or yesterday, I'll have it posted by my devoted friends. Cigarette 1, cigarette 2, cigarette 3, one two three, one plus two plus three equals six cigarettes; one smoked, another grilled, and the third roasted on the spit before the fire. The hands hanging at the neck of the rope which was let down in a rush from the tree which flies away, whip to their heart's content her pure Venus of a body which is most unshapely. Rough-shod, the day lowers the weight of her years into the shady well. The guts which Pegasus drags behind him after the fight draw her portrait on the whiteness and hardness of the gleaming marble of her sorrow.

The noise of the unfastened shutters, hitting their drunken bells on the crumpled sheets of the stones, tears despairing cries of pleasure from the night. The hammer blows of flowers and the lovely stench of her tresses season the stew with her bay leaves and cloves. Flying hands, hands detached from the lace sleeves of her bodice so carefully folded and placed on the velvet of the arm-chair, leaning so harshly against the cheeks of the axe planted, mournfully on the block, copy the lesson which they have learnt in a fine round hand. Hard rock of the anemones devouring the quicklime of the curtain asleep on the ladder leaning against the sulphur of the sky hung in the window-frame. The most valid reasons, the imminence of peril, and the fears and desires which drive her on, do not at a time like this keep her from the sullen joy of comfortably installing herself on the hope-green sofa.


TART

[enters running]

Good morning! Good evening! I'm bringing you an orgy. I'm stark naked and I'm dying of thirst. Hurry up and make me a cup of tea and some honey roasts. I'm as hungry as a wolf and I'm so warm! Let me make myself comfortable. Give me a fur filled with hair full of moths so that I can cover myself. And first kiss me on the mouth and here and here here here and there and everywhere. It must be that I love you to have come in this sloppy way, as a neighbour and stark naked to say hallo to you and to make you believe that you love me and want to have me against you, cute little lover that I am for you and absolute mistress of my thoughts of you, who seem to be such a tender adorer of my charms. Don't be so upset, give me another nice kiss. And a thousand more. Go on now, go and make me some tea. And meanwhile I'm going to cut the corn on my little toe that's annoying me. [BIG FOOT *takes her in his arms and they fall to the floor.*]


### TART

[*getting up after the embrace*]

You've got quite a way of receiving and taking. I'm covered with snow and I'm shivering. Bring me a hot brick. [*He goes out. She squats in front of the prompter's box, with her face to the audience, grimaces for a good ten minutes*] Ouf! that's better! [*She blows, blows again, tidies up her hair, sits down on the floor and starts skilfully demolishing her toes.*]


### BIG FOOT

[*enters holding a big account-book under his arm.*]

Here's your tea. No water in the tap. No tea. No sugar. No cup or saucer. No spoon. No glass. No bread and no jam. But I've got a nice surprise for you here under my arm: *my novel*, and I'm going to cut you a few slices from this big sausage and I'm going to cram them into your head, if you allow me and want to listen to me very attentively during these few long years of dark night which we have to spend blithely this morning until noon. Here's page 380,000 which seems to me seriously interesting. [*He reads:*] "The pungent odour spread around the concrete fact established *a priori* of the tale does not involve any deduction for the character intended for this work. Before his wife and in the presence of a notary, we, the only responsible party established and known as an honourably known author, I engage my entire responsibility only in the specific cases where my excessive anxieties may become obsessive and murderous for the partial view of the person who is being interviewed, spouting at full blast the plumb line of the complicated machine for determining at all costs on the exact findings of the case already experimented upon by others, contrary to the light shed by the viewpoints on which the weight of the internal specifications rests." "The armed ballroom was full of the sugar and the brine of the beautiful and the best of the high select society seated before the accomplished fact full of the bronzed feathers of the children thrown to the winds like belated and worm-eaten tears." "On the regimental steeple, the clock displayed the most complete indifference to the angles of the sun-dial held at its waist The titillations of crows, making the notched wheels of the machine for sewing and unsewing buttons, liven up the half-dead landscape so little that the grass grows on their flight and the shadows thrown by their wings do not stick to the wall of the church but slide along the cobblestones of the square, where they break to pieces in a satisfactory realization of the adventure destined to occupy this temporary pigeon hole."

[*entering*]

Oy. . . . We're bringing you shrimps! Oy, oy, we're bringing you shrimps!

### BIG FOOT

That's delightful! Here we are having a quiet chat and you come bothering us with your lousy shrimps. Onion, and you, Cousin, what the devil do you want us to do with your shrimps?

### ONION

That'll teach me to offer you shrimps next time.

### BIG FOOT

No but sometimes. . . .

### THE COUSIN

You, Tart, I'm going off right this moment to tell your mother everything. That's a fine how d'ye do! All naked in front of a gentleman, a writer, a poet . . . and all naked with stockings on, it may be very highbrow and very naughty but it doesn't make for either a Venus or a muse or the sort of behaviour befitting a self-respecting girl. And what's your mother going to say when she learns at the wash-house this evening of your deplorable, shameless behaviour as if you were a prostitute who'd been dragged into the sewer of *Big Foot's Artist's Studio* by wanton desires?

### TART

Cousin, you're going a bit too far. . . . And, by the way, do you have some cotton or lend me your handkerchief?

[ 49 ]

I'm going to tidy up and go. I'm leaving. I'm going back to the house. Really, that man is a pig, a pervert, a fop, and a skunk. [*She goes into the bathroom.*]

### BIG FOOT

Now that Tart's gone, listen to me. That girl is crazy and she's trying to take us in with her phony airs of a princess. I love her, of course, and I'm enjoying myself. But because of that to make her my wife, my muse, or my Venus, there is a long and hard path to come. If her beauty excites me and her stench drives me wild, her way of eating at the table, of dressing and her mannered manners give me a pain in the neck. Now frankly, tell me what you think. I'm listening. You, Cousin, what do *you* think?

### THE COUSIN

I know that girl friend of yours very well. We were at school together for a few years. And I assure you that in class her conduct was held up to us as an example. If she was covered with pimples, of course I know it wasn't her fault but the lack of various fats and the free-and-easiness of a girl who abandoned herself to her instincts. Physically very dirty, unkempt, reeking with a thousand bad smells, and drowsy. In her short black pinafore, her big bedroom slippers, and her knitted cape, all the men—old workmen, young fellows and gentry—we could see in their eyes the fires and candles lit up before the devastating image of her that they carried away, burning in their hands which were hidden in their pockets the pure diamond of the Fountain of Youth.

ONION

For me that kid had the flavour of angelica.

THE COUSIN

No doubt about it! Tart is a big and very lovely girl.

BIG FOOT

Her body is a summer night overflowing with the light and perfume of jasmine and stars.

ONION

You like her, Big Foot. Big Foot, that's your affair. If you like her, fine, and you can have the happiness and the headaches. Keep your chin up! My blessings upon you. And good and long luck! Are you coming, Cousin? We'll be going. Eh! Big Foot, no hard feelings. . . . About the shrimps, above all, don't forget to put in a big piece of bacon fat, some parsley, and a good glassful of asses' milk.

THE COUSIN

So long, Big Foot! [*They go out.*]

BIG FOOT

What an awful pack of dopes! [*He lies down on the bed and starts to write.*] "The soft blue of the bow which, with its veil of lace, covers the roses of the nude body of the amaranth of the oat field, mops up drop by drop the burden of little bells from the shoulders of lemon yellow beating his wings. The maidens of Avignon already have thirty-three long years of their annuity."

[ 51 ]

## TART

*[comes out of the bathroom all dressed and wearing a hat of the latest style]*

What, have they gone? Without saying a word. French leave. Shall I tell you what, all those people disgust me! You're the only one I love. But we're going to have to be good, my great big everything.

## BIG FOOT

*[stretched out on his bed and looking underneath]*

I'm carrying in my torn pocket the sugar-candy umbrella of the unfolded angles of the black light of the sun.

*Curtain.*

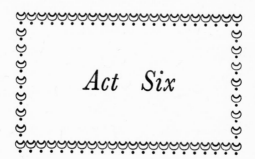

Act Six

### SKINNY ANGUISH

The burn made by my unhealthy passions irritates the soreness of the chilblains which are enamoured of the prism permanently set up on the bronze-coloured angles of the rainbow and evaporates it into confetti. I am only the congealed soul stuck to the panes of the fire. I beat my portrait against my brow and hawk the merchandise of my grief at the windows which are closed to all mercy. My shirt, torn to shreds by the rigid fans of my tears, bites with the nitric acid of its blows, the sea-weed of my arms dragging the dress from my feet and my cries from door to door. The little bag of pralines which I bought from Big Foot yesterday for 0 francs 40 centimes is burning my hands. A purulent fistula in my heart, love is playing marbles between the feathers of its wings. The old sewing-machine which turns the horses and the lions of the dishevelled merry-go-round of my desires chops up my sausage flesh and offers it alive to the icy hands of the still-born stars which are rapping their wolfish hunger and their oceanic thirst at my window-panes. The enormous pile of logs awaits its fate with resignation. Let's make the soup. [*Reading from a cook-book:*] A half-quarter of Spanish melon, palm oil, lemon, kidney-beans, salt, vinegar, bread-crumbs; cook with a low flame; from time to time delicately take a soul in agony out of purgatory; cool it; reproduce a thousand copies on imperial Japanese vellum and allow to chill long enough to be able to give it to the octopuses. Sister! Sister! Come here! Come help me set the table and fold the dirty linen spotted with blood! Hurry up, sister, the soup's already cold and is cracking at the bottom of the glass of the mirror-wardrobe. The whole afternoon I've been embroidering a thousand stories into this soup that it will whisper secretly in your ear, if you want to keep for the end the architecture of the skeleton's bouquet of violets.

### FAT ANGUISH

[*uncombed and filthy dirty, getting out of the sheets of the bed which is full of fried potatoes, holding an old frying-pan in her hand*]

I've come from far away and am dazzled by the great patience that I had, to follow behind the hearse jumping like the carp which the fat dyer and cleaner who's so scrupulous about his accounts wanted to lay at my feet.

### SKINNY ANGUISH

The sun.

### FAT ANGUISH

Love.

### SKINNY ANGUISH

You're so lovely!

### FAT ANGUISH

When I left the sewer of our house this morning, immediately, two steps from the gate, I took my pair of hobnailed boots off my wings, and, leaping into the icy pond of my griefs, I let myself be dragged by the waves far from the banks. Lying on my back, I stretched out on the scum of this water and I kept my mouth open for a long time in order to catch my tears. My closed eyes also caught the crown of that long rain of flowers.

Dinner is served.

FAT ANGUISH

Hurray for joy, love, and springtime!

SKINNY ANGUISH

Come along, carve the turkey and take plenty of stuffing. The big bouquet of horrors and frights is already waving farewell. And the mussel shells are clacking their teeth, scared to death under the icy ears of boredom. [*She takes a piece of bread which she soaks in the sauce.*] This hash needs salt and pepper. My aunt had a canary which used to sing old drinking-songs all night long.

FAT ANGUISH

I'm taking some more sturgeon. The pungent flavour of these dishes keeps my depraved tastes for spicy and indigestible foods in a state of high suspense.

SKINNY ANGUISH

I just found the lace dress I wore at the white ball given on that baleful day, my birthday, all moth-eaten and full of spots on top of the cupboard in the lavatory, writhing in inflamed pain beneath the dust of the tick-tock of the grandfather clock. It's certainly our char who put it on the other day to go and see her boy-friend.

FAT ANGUISH

Look, the door is running forward. There's someone inside who's coming in. The postman? No, it's Tart. [*Addressing* TART.] Come in. Come have tea with us. How pleased you must be. Tell us the news about Big

Foot. Onion arrived this morning pale and drawn, soaking wet and wounded, with his forehead pierced through and through by a pickaxe. He was crying. We attended to him and consoled him as well as we could. But he was in pieces. He was bleeding everywhere and was screaming incoherent words like a lunatic.

### SKINNY ANGUISH

You know, the cat had her kittens last night.

### FAT ANGUISH

We drowned them in a hard stone, to be exact, in a beautiful amethyst. The weather was fine this morning. A bit cold, but warm just the same.

### TART

You know, I met love. He has scraped knees and he begs from door to door. He doesn't have a sou and is looking for a job as conductor on a suburban bus. It's sad, but go and help him . . . he'll turn on you and sting you. Big Foot wanted to have me and he's the one who got caught in the trap. Look: I stayed out in the sun too long I'm covered with blisters. Love. Love. Here's a five-franc piece, change it into dollars for me and keep the crumbs of small change. Good-bye! For ever! Happy holiday, friends! Good night! A very good day to you! Happy New Year and farewell! [*She lifts up her skirt, and laughing, leaps with one bound through the window breaking all the panes.*]

### FAT ANGUISH

A beautiful girl, intelligent, but peculiar. All this is going to come to no good end.

#### SKINNY ANGUISH

Let's call all these people. [*She takes a trumpet and blows the "Fall In". All the characters in the play come running up.*] You, Onion, step forward. You have a right to six drawing-room chairs. Here they are.

#### ONION

Thank you, Madame!

#### FAT ANGUISH

You, Big Foot, if you can answer my questions, I'll give you the hanging lamp in the dining-room. Tell me how much are four and four?

#### BIG FOOT

Much too much and not a great deal.

#### SKINNY ANGUISH

Very good!

#### FAT ANGUISH

Very good!

#### SKINNY ANGUISH

[*uncorking a bottle and putting it under his nose*]
What does that smell of? [ROUND END *laughs*.]

#### SKINNY ANGUISH

Very good! You understood. Here's a box full of pens. They're for you. And good luck.

#### FAT ANGUISH

Tart, give us your accounts.

#### TART

I've got Ham. Tripe, Salami. Blood sausage. And my hair covered with chipolatas. I've got mauve gums, sugar in my water, and my gouty hands full of the white of eggs. Bony cavities. Bile, ulcers, Fistulas, the King's evil. And lips twisted with honey and marshmallows. Decently dressed, clean, I wear with elegance the ridiculous clothes that are given to me. I'm a mother and a perfect tart, and I can dance the rhumba.

SKINNY ANGUISH

You get a can of petrol and a fishing-rod. But first, you have to dance with all of us. Start with Big Foot. [*The music plays and they all dance changing from partner to partner every moment.*]

BIG FOOT

Let's wrap the worn-out sheets in the angels' face powder and let's turn the mattress inside out in the brambles. Let's light all the lanterns. Let's throw the flights of doves against the bullets with all our might and let's close the houses that have been demolished by the bombs, with a double lock.

[*All the characters stop moving on both sides of the stage. Opening the window at the back of the room with a single movement, a golden sphere as tall as a man enters. It lights up the whole room and blinds the characters, who take handkerchiefs out of their pockets and bandage their eyes and, stretching out their right arms, point at one another, all crying out at the same time and several times:*]

You! You! You!

[*On the big golden sphere appear the letters of the word:*]
Nobody.

*Curtain.*

# DATE DUE